A
IS FOR AUSTRALIA

John Brennan

Houghton Mifflin
Australia

Aa

is for Australia, of course.

Bb

is for billy,
a tin for making tea
or cooking over a camp-fire.

Cc

is for cubby-house,
a special place where kids
can hide and play.

Dd

is for dingo,
a wild dog that howls but cannot bark.

Ee

**is for emus,
large birds that run very fast
but cannot fly.**

Ff

is for fishing
the pier with
your dad.

Gg

is for gum-nuts,
the woody cups
that hold the seeds
of Eucalyptus trees.

is for harvester,
a huge machine for reaping wheat,
oats, barley and other crops.

**is for ice-cream,
so cold on your tongue.**

JJ

is for joey,
a young kangaroo,
safe in its mother's pouch
until it grows big enough
to look after itself.

KK

is for koala,
a furry animal
that looks like
a Teddy bear
and eats gum-leaves.

LI

is for Luna Park,
a fun-fair with rides and games and fairy-floss.

Mm

is for milk bar,
the local shop where you can buy
drinks, lollies and groceries.

is for nugget,
a lump of solid gold.
You might find one in the ground,
or in a river, if you are very lucky.

Oo

is for the Opera House,
a famous building on Sydney Harbour
where you can go to see acting, singing and dancing.

Pp

is for possum,
with its big, round eyes
and long tail.
At night you sometimes
hear possums rustling
in the trees, or thumping
on the roof of
your house.

Qq

is for quokkas,
short-tailed wallabies
that live in
Western Australia.

Rr

is for rosella,
a brightly-coloured parrot
that you see in gardens
and in the bush.

Ss

is for stockman,
who rounds up the cattle on his horse.

Tt

is for tram,
which carries people around the streets of Melbourne.
It runs on rails like a train,
but shares the road with the cars.

Uu

is for Uluru,
an Aboriginal name
for the huge rock
at the centre of Australia.
It is also called
Ayers Rock.

Vv

is for Vegemite,
a favourite taste
with Australian kids.

USE BY
NOV 84
VEGEMITE
CONCENTRATED YEAST EXTRACT
455 g NET
KRAFT*
* TRADE MARK
5g OF THIS FOOD CONTAINS: VITAMIN B1 0·55 mg, RIBOFLAVIN 0·80 mg, NIACIN 5·50 mg
WHICH ARE HALF THE AVERAGE DAILY ALLOWANCES.
PRODUCT OF AUSTRALIA
FOR AFTER SCHOOL SNACKS
SPREAD ON BUTTERED BISCUITS
VEGEMITE

WW

is for windmill, which pumps up water from under the ground in paddocks and near farm houses.

Xx

is the sign for a railway crossing.
It warns drivers to watch out for trains
where the road crosses the train tracks.

Yy

is for yabbies,
little crayfish that live
in dams and creeks.
You can catch them
with meat tied to the
end of a bit of string.
They are good to eat.

Zz

is for zinc cream,
which stops you getting
a sunburnt nose
on the beach in summer.

Houghton Mifflin Australia Pty Ltd
112 Lewis Road, Knoxfield, Victoria, 3180
PO Box 289, Ferntree Gully, Victoria, 3156

First published 1984 J.M. Dent Pty Limited
Reprinted 1985

Re-Issued 1989 by Hougton Mifflin Australia

National Library of Australia
Cataloguing-in-Publication Data

Brennan, John, 1952-
  A is for Australia.

  For children.
  ISBN 0 86 770 101 3

  1. English language — Alphabet —
  Juvenile literature. I. Title.
421'.1

Designed by John Nicholson
Produced by P·I·X·E·L Publishing
Typeset by Meredith Typesetters,
Melbourne

Printed in Hong Kong by
South China Printing Company (1988) Limited

John Brennan is a freelance photographer who lives in Melbourne with Leonie, his wife and their children, Patrick and Rosemary.

The author would like to thank the following people and organisations for their help in the making of this book: Leonie Keaney, Rosalind Price, Andrew and Sarah James, Sam and Eve Brennan, Sarah and Nicholas Higginbottom, Brian Trotman, Kylie Poon, Ben Noonan, Anthony Leong, Robyn Freestone, Alan Streeter, Anna Owens, Jan Ferguson and the children of Grade 2/3 from Bell Primary School, Melbourne, the Royal Melbourne Zoo, Healesville Sanctuary, and Taronga Zoo, Sydney.